Excerpts from

www.youngfunandcathoic.blogspot.www.

Encouraging Words Blog by Lisa Hendrix Simmons

2013-2014

Encouraging Words

By Lisa Hendrix Simmons

"A compliment can truly be all that stands between someone being successful and giving up. Stand in that gap and offer an encouraging word."

Brett & Kate McKay,

Art of Manliness

Just what in the world is E-Word? E stands for "Encouraging" and since that word is long, I've shortened it to a cute little internet savy letter. So now, this year, each week you can ask each other, "Oh, have you said your E-word yet?

E-Word isn't just a word. It can be a phrase, compliment or otherwise nice thing to say to someone. This year's weekly blog entry will be about encouraging other people.

I was reading an article on the Art of Manliness site (www.artofmanliness.www) how humans are more wired to hear negative things than the positive things.

For example, you could compliment someone on their hair, dress, shoes, purse, and jewelry and then tell them they have a smudge on their eyelid, they will remember you said something about the smudge on their eyelid!

No, really it's true! Somebody, somewhere, not me, got paid to do a study on this! Anyway, the point is supposedly we hear more negative things and react to them than we hear the compliments. The solution is to try to even out this terrible travesty of human interaction by giving meaningful compliments to people, family members, co-workers, someone you meet in a store.

It must be well meant, and no back handed compliment either, which is NOT a compliment to begin with in case that's all you ever give!

So now you can use the jingle, "Have you said your E-Word today?" Or, "Hey, what's your E-Word?"

Okay, I digress, but I am challenging you to a year of Encouraging Words to others! Compliment someone on their manners, or the job they are doing. It doesn't have to be hard, but it does have to sound true. No faking here people!

Think about how when you get a compliment, doesn't it make you float for a few minutes? Someone compliments my singing and I get through at least half a day forgetting what a pain the computer was or how the copier jammed up again.

Try it, you will see it helps you feel better when you see that person light up. And if they don't, keep doing it, take your encouraging word wherever you go. Go on! You can do it, I know you can. You are so good at helping people feel good and positive about themselves! I really like that about you!

And we are off, in week two of a brand new year. Yay us! This year's new theme, finding encouraging words to use is something like being a positive person. So it has a two-fold purpose this year. Not only helping us become more positive people by looking for good things in other people, but also, actually letting others know they are being good people too. And to quote one of my fave characters in the movie, "Sahara", "It's like a two for one deal, which I always think is better!"

Just this morning I received an encouraging word, or rather an encouraging email. A Girl Scout leader emailed me asking me to speak to her group about writing and how I develop my characters in my fiction writing. Nothing could have started my day better than being asked to talk about how to write books! I love getting kids excited about writing! So by her simple request, I had an awesome morning, first feeling a qualification for my writing skills and second, getting asked to encourage kids to do something I love doing: writing!

Sometimes that's all it takes to make someone's day.

But according to the article on Encouraging Words at www.artofmanliness.com there is a list of reasons why we don't compliment or give encouraging words to other people more. This is the list:

1. OUR BRAINS ARE DESIGNED TO FOCUS ON THE NEGATIVE

2. YOU ARE SELF ABSORBED: Most of us are more concerned about our own performance or behavior than if someone else messes up or performs poorly.

3. YOU SEE EVERYTHING AS A COMPETITION. Some of us, (including myself, I know, cough...ouch) see everything in life as a competition, or at least something we have to be able to do well. And sometimes it's hard to tell someone else THEY have done a better job at something than we have, like writing an awesome article. (your brain is noodling why can't I get published like they just did?) See what I mean?

So we neglect to give compliments because it is admitting they are better than we are, when in actuality you are the perfect person to give the compliment BECAUSE you write too and know the value of a job well done! I didn't say it this competition would make sense, just that it happens to the best of us!

4. YOU ARE SHY - no really. It's like making cold calls in sales. It's hard to just walk up to someone and say, "Hey nice job." Or even worse explain why you thought it was a good job.

5. YOU DON'T WANT TO LOOK LIKE A SUCK-UP OR BROWN-NOSER. Enough said.

6. YOU ASSUME THEY ALREADY KNOW they did a good job, wrote a great paper, sang a great song, whatever. And honestly, even if they do already know that, it wouldn't hurt to remind them. I know I can sing decently, but it never hurts to be reminded because back to that competition thing, you are always thinking you have do better or that everyone is better than you and you have to keep trying harder.

7. And last but not least, YOU DON'T KNOW WHAT TO SAY. IF you avoid giving compliments because you don't know what to say then keep reading these suggestions in the next several months!

I missed a perfect opportunity today to give a compliment and I blame it on #4. I truly was shy. I didn't know this person and I felt funny just walking up to her and giving her a compliment. So I have a lot to learn by working on this year of Encouraging Words myself.

So, this week, your mission is to go through your day, and if you encounter someone doing something positive or whatever, practice your encouraging word by saying something to them. Even telling the store bagger to have a great day and thanks for bagging your groceries, is enough to count this week. Hey, it's baby steps, man!

Good luck and way to go for reading all the way through this week's blog. Maybe you should begin blogging too, you already like to read, why not take it a step further and write down your ideas on encouraging words? You can even type a comment below. It may be the first time but that doesn't matter! The hardest part is beginning!

Dearest God,

I know I drive people crazy by obsessively worrying about them. I know I have to leave them alone to make their own decisions. I know I have to stop using my fears to manipulate them into doing things they don't want to do.

There I've said it. Now I just need to act on it. That's where you come in God. Please help me to detach with love from the ones I love, and leave them in your protective care. You know what's best for them so much more than I do.

So I pray that your will be done, not mine. Help me to love them in a way that will be supportive without stifling, encouraging without overpowering and concerned but not controlling.

Lord, I pray you'll lead them in your ways and keep them safely under your wing.

Allia Zobel Nolan

This week we're talking about giving compliments, the how-to, that is! I read in the Art of Manliness article that to overcome our negative and egocentric biases, we need to harness our inner Sherlock Holmes by observing more frequently and more keenly.

Nicely put, because sometimes I am truly more focused on my problems or the world as I see it, to notice other people having a new haircut, new outfit or whatever. I don't consider myself a selfish person, but I realize I do focus more on my shortcomings and worry about other people's opinions of them, than I do on complimenting others and looking for good things. While I don't go around criticizing people to their faces, I also don't make a point of handing out compliments on a daily basis either. Somewhere between these two things is where I want to be.

So to begin, start on small stuff. Just this morning I was getting out of the car and the student in the next car had on one of those really cute knitted hats, the kind that has ear flaps, was pink and had big eyes on the top! Normally I would have thought to myself, how cute and giggled. But this morning, working on my Encouraging Words, I actually spoke up and told her she had on a really cute hat!

She smiled shyly and muttered, "Thanks!"

Sure my compliment was a really small thing, but it was a start! The thing about compliments is they have to be sincere. If you roll your eyes while complimenting someone's clothing, they may get the idea you are making fun of them. I remember those teen years too much, but it happened a lot then. Nice "Peace" t-shirt, Lisa" *giggle, snort.* Those kinds of compliments we DON'T need these days. But one that really makes another person feel good about something they've chosen to wear is a winner.

The other thing about compliments is it helps if they are specific. Instead of saying, "You look nice today." It helps more to say, "Wow, that purple color looks really good on you!" or "That sweater really brings the blue out in your eyes!" help the compliment-getter to know you are really paying attention.

So give it a try this week and see how it goes! Don't over do it, you might get too giddy from all the adrenaline! But try giving out a compliment a day if you can. See how it makes the other person look and feel, and how it gets you out of your self focused rut! Good luck!

We shall find peace. We shall hear angels. We shall never know all the good that a simple smile can do.

- Mother Teresa

Let a smile be your umbrella! I love smiling. I confess I don't always do it and am very bad about not having a poker face. But smiling truly is the best ice breaker, best non-verbal communication, best day maker, best everything hands down.

Who doesn't like a smile? (And we are not talking about the evil smiles which aren't smiles, just a turning up of the corners of your mouth.)

A smile is like an encouraging word without talking. Sometimes there is nothing you can say or do and a smile does it for you. Even at sad times there is a smile you use that is full of compassion and care for another person.

Smiles comes not only from your mouth, but from your eyes, in fact that is how you recognize a true smile, in the eyes.

This week, let some extra smiles be your encouraging words to others. Even if you aren't feeling very encouraged yourself, or are down. A smile put out in the world almost always is reflected back to you. Or as I have experienced, you'll receive a surprised look after flashing a bright wide smile at someone who wasn't expecting one!

Go ahead, make my day: Smile!

You are never too old to set another goal or

to dream a new dream.
- C. S. Lewis

Last week while getting some blood work done, I was asked not once but twice within a few minutes time if I was over the age of 55. Now I know better than to get upset at questions by medical personnel who see people all the time, coming and going so they aren't really looking past the silver hair of a woman who sits down across from them, but gosh it upset me! I mean I have two more LONG years before I turn 55!!!! Come on!!!!

But I let those comments get to me. It didn't help that I was there because my blood pressure had been running a tad bit high and I wanted to find out what was going on. So of course my BP didn't look really great after those comments either.

Later while I'm going reading the news I see a blog that listed activities you should not engage in if you are over 50 including: *Parkour*, mosh pit surfing, and drinking champagne out of shoes. I still engage in martial arts and sparring and ground combat so I took offense at the Parkour restriction. I love low range *Parkour* and even practice it! Did you see me trip over the curb in Target's parking lot last week and do a perfect roll? I was doing Parkour off cars and curbs long before it became a hit in James Bond movies!

But I did begin to realize that my Encouraging Words blog this year was going to have to really hit home with me if I was going to get my blood pressure back in the normal range. Life has been extremely stressed out lately and knew I was letting it happen to me. "Let Go and Let God" is always my motto, but that doesn't mean I live it all the time! I have those "Mom" worries and anxieties with kids out of the nest with one almost two thousand miles away, the other figuring out where she is going next, a full time job and a family business to run. If I sound like a broken record I apologize but I think sometimes we women think we can just keep adding stuff to our plates and the plate won't break.

We need to think of our plates as paper not china. And we have to take care of the plate, not just the food that is on it! Even if our plates are fine china they have a load limit!

Anyway, Encouraging Words need to help lift us up to the funny in life, the less stressed way of looking at the anxiety causing events that grab on like Velcro and try harder to laugh our way to old age.

And it is never too old to begin anything new! There are hundreds of examples of people starting over, beginning a new hobby or doing something different as they age. There are a lot of young people just sitting around with high BP's too and they need to get out and try some hardcore *Parkour* too, even if it's just the parking lot curb tripping you up!

"I find letters from God dropt in the street and every one of them is signed by God's name."

- Walt Whitman

"Go confidently in the direction of your dreams. Live the life you have imagined." ~ Henry David Thoreau

Ever since I was eight years old, I have dreamed of being a writer. I imagined all kinds of stories in my head, I wore out thousands of pencils, collected notebooks, paper, yellow legal pads, any kind of writing pad I could find and wrote stories. They were mostly stories that include myself as the heroine. I didn't use my own name of course, but I lived through the characters in my stories and I was going to make a living being a writer some day!

I asked for a typewriter for Christmas when I was ten and received it. I can still smell the ink ribbon, see the gray and red case, feel the touch of the keys as I happily spent summer inside living adventure after adventure in the bedroom I shared with my two sisters.

First, I was off on a mystery, then it was to the bottom of the sea with the sailors from Voyage to the Bottom of the Sea, to rescuing people as a teen paramedic with Johnny and Roy on Emergency! I didn't realize it at the time, but I was writing screenplays for television shows I was watching. I invented my own plots, action and dialog.

Then it was on to my own style of fiction as I created characters not seen on television or movies. They were of my own invention, romances, westerns, pirates and princesses. Some summers I even went as far as to put on "plays" with my stories, begging my sisters and neighborhood friends to act out while I directed and even recorded on my tape recorder the shootouts in my westerns!

I wrote plays for my classmates to perform in English class which they enjoyed because we all would get extra credit! As I moved into high school I was including some of my closest friends in my adventures, changing the names to protect the innocent, but they were included in on the adventure stories that way too. And they enjoyed reading them.

Disappointed that the college I chose to attend did not have a writing major, I instead majored in English and Journalism. I would still get to write, not the fun adventure stuff, but it was helpful as I learned to deepen my descriptions, write good concise paragraphs and question everything I included in my stories, "was this really needed for the plot, will my reader understand it?"

When I got married and began having kids, the urge to write was no lesser than when I was eight and I began to write stories for my children. They were adventures and one character in particular began to emerge, a young woman who was studying as a martial artist and bodyguard: Kip MacAllister!

On a trip to a bookstore I received a coupon for a Print On Demand publisher online. I found out I could upload my story and have it printed and bound in a book of my very own, without going through editors and copyreaders who either didn't like my stories or wanted to make big changes to them with still no guarantee of publishing them.

I was in heaven! I began publishing my Kip MacAllister books for my kids. I only ordered copies for them and my family to read. But teachers at the school where I worked found out I was writing and asked for copies. Soon my books were in the school library and I was invited to talk to students at other schools about writing and my books.

Just recently, while visiting with some cousins, I found out they were ordering my books for their kids to read. I was thrilled!! I may not be rich and famous, but I am living the dream I've had since I was eight years old: I was a writer!

You never know when an encouraging word may come along in your life and keep your dreams alive.

In my life, it's when my parents bought me the typewriter so I could make more real looking books.

It was teacher's encouraging me by letting me put on plays in English class.

It was being asked to be a reporter for my college newspaper and seeing my byline in print.

It was my husband who would put the kids to bed at night so I could have "writing time" and who also encouraged me to use the coupon for the POD publishing and he has been my biggest supporter in addition to my parents, siblings and my own children in becoming a writer.

It still seems funny to call myself a writer. But as I get older and realize I have written a lot of things. I have learned I always have to have a pencil, pen, notebook, laptop, or thumb drive with me at all times in case an idea comes to me. I write copy for our church bulletin, I write a bi-monthly 8 page newsletter for our parish's youth, I write monthly Family Faith inserts for our church bulletin, and website copy. I can't get away from writing and I wouldn't have it any other way.

My husband described me best one time when I was worrying I was spending too much time writing my stories instead of doing housework, he said, "Lisa, you are the real you when you are writing! You need to write!"

Those encouraging words are what kept me writing all these years and now I encourage other people to write! I love talking to kids about writing and character development!

Encouraging words – at their best! Let them take you off on your dreams!

"I'd rather be a could-be if I cannot be an are; because a could-be is a maybe who is reaching for a star, I'd rather be a has-been than a might-have-been, by far; for a might have-been has never been, but a has was once an are."

~ Milton Berle, Comedian and Actor

Encouraging words are what make us who we are. I love the quote repeated by Milton Berle. It not only is encouraging, but it is a statement to sticking to things in life, even if you can't be the best, most important or highly paid something, you can at least BE SOMETHING! If for no other reason than you tried.

If you never try something, whether it's a new job, a new hobby or making yourself a better person, how will you ever look back and say, "Hey I did that!" How will you create memories?

Encouraging words help us along but they don't put us in the end result. WE have to do that. We use encouraging words like the chalk that rock climbers use. They still have to use arm and leg power, and the ropes and pitons, but that bit of chalk is what keeps their hands from sweating and loosing a grip on the rope.

While dangling from a 40 foot high, two foot across platform in the midst of tree, I had to swing out with only my feet still on the platform, my arms holding on a rope and lower myself to the stable ground below. Think I needed an encouraging word or two then? You bet! It took me a long time to do it, I didn't trust my arms to hold the rope tight enough to keep from plummeting to the ground. But since there was no other way down and with my husband and kids encouraging me, I finally said a prayer and swung out into space. Whew...I still didn't like it, but I survived and slowly let the rope slip through the pulley system and gently dropped to the leave covered earth below. All in one piece.

Encouraging words, everyone needs them at many times in life!

Adieu!

I came across an interesting tidbit of information today. And I guess if I had studied French instead of the one year of Spanish I took I might have known this. The French word, *"Adieu"* which everyone uses when they are saying goodbye to someone, quite literally means, "*to God"*. In other words, when you say, *"Adieu*!" to someone while waving, you are leaving them in God's care.

That was stunning to me. How wonderful! Of course the other words we use to assure a safe journey or see you again later also mean go with God too like "*Good-bye,*" good - comes from God. "*Vaya con dios*" in Spanish means this too.

Sometimes we forget to stop and think about putting another person in God's care. The very send off we have repeated for years does just that. How beautiful! Too bad we sometimes shorten our *Good-Bye* to just *'bye!* or worse yet, "*See 'ya*!"

Maybe for Lent practice actually using the full "go with God at your side" send off. I know it makes me feel better to remind them AND me I am trusting them to God's care!

Happy Lent!

Live with intention
Walk to the edge
Listen hard
Practice wellness
LAUGH
Choose with no regret
Appreciate your friends
Continue to learn
Do what you love

Live every day – get over the sadness, smile, leave as friends, forget the anger, no grudges, give hugs, RESOLVE TO BE HAPPY!

No matter what else goes on in your life, resolving to be happy is the most important thing you can do for yourself and your family and friends.

I don't mean the kind of happy you get from having no worries, plenty of money, fame or fortune.

Nope, I mean the kind of happy that sings in your soul. Also known in some circles as JOY.

Joy doesn't get much press. The only time you hear much about the word JOY is at Christmas when we sing "Joy To the World." And just what is Joy to the World?

Do you bring joy to your world? Do people see you and smile or melt into the wall? Do people think of you as a joyful person?

I know people, even very religious people, who can suck the joy out of Mass by the way approach life: it's one big sigh after another. That's not joy.

Joy is what wells up inside you, it can happen when you see a baby smile for the first time, or get up early and spot the most beautiful sunrise you've ever seen! Joy bubbles up from your soul, you can't explain it, it's just there, fizzing and bubbling like a freshly opened can of soda!

Joy takes choosing to live your life so others see the Christ in you. Christ had joy. He exuded it everywhere He went. It's why so many people were attracted to Him. He didn't have to wave a banner, hand out business cards or yell, "Gather round, miracle about to happen!"

Jesus had a natural joy that came from knowing He was from the Father, and the Father was in Him.

We know the Father too, and the Father dwells in us. Why don't we show our joy like Jesus did?

We still have time in Lent to work on showing our joy. Go for it! Make a joyful noise and shout "Joy to the world!"

"Throw back the shoulders, let the heart sing, let the eyes flash, let the mind be lifted up, look upward and say to yourself... Nothing is impossible!"

- Norman Vincent Peale

Joy!

Even though it's Lent and we may be thinking of pain, sorrow, of giving up instead of getting, let's not get mired down in the mud of fasting and ashes. What Lent truly is about is learning to look at the JOY in our lives.

What our fasting can do for us is clean out our spirits; make room once again for the JOY that God has given us to live. We get so bogged down by the day to day struggles, making ends meet, working the job, cleaning the house, taking care of the kids, our friends, parents, our Church, that our Joy is depleted and we forget to fill it up again.

During Lent, maybe what we need is not to concentrate so much on fasting as drudgery again, but as a clean up of sorts. Just like when you finally had enough of the dust bunnies, the finger prints in the dust around on the shelves, that dirty spot on the kitchen floor we still haven't cleaned up, JOY during Lent can enliven our hearts again, lift us up above all the day to day making do.

Joy, Joy, JOY!!! It's a word that is so encouraging. The mere mention of the word joy cannot be taken in any other way than to celebrate the fact that God loves YOU! And your heart wells up inside because none of your other problems matter. All that spiritual dryness we experience in life can be refreshed again if we truly look at the joy in our lives.

So what if your job is horrible right now, your friends or co-workers are crabby. They can't steal your JOY!

"Joy always springs from a certain outlook on man and on God." When your eye is sound, your body too is filled with Light. The vocation to happiness always passes through the channels of knowledge and love, of contemplation and action. This attainment of such an outlook is not just a matter of psychology. It is also a fruit of the Holy Spirit. Jesus had joy because the Spirit who dwelt fully in him made his earthly life so alert to the joys of daily life, so tactful and persuasive for putting sinners back on the road to a new youth of heart and mind. It is the same Spirit who animated the blessed Virgin and each of the saints. It is the Spirit of Pentecost who leads those living today to be followers of Christ." (excerpt from *Gaudete in Domino* Pope Paul VI – 1975)

So live your JOY! Clean out your heart this Lenten season. Let your joy bubble up in you! Look at the day and see how you can let your light shine!

Thousands of candles can be lit from a single candle, and the life of the candle will not be shortened. Happiness never decreases by being shared.
- The Buddha

Many years back, my sister-in-law was pregnant with her third child and I was already raising three kids all of whom were in grade school at this time. I remember her asking me "how do you divide your love between three kids?"

Somehow the Holy Spirit intervened because I am not known for my eloquence in speech, just ask anyone in my family, because I actually answered, "It doesn't divide, it multiplies!"

And it's true. As the years have gone on I never felt my love was divided between my husband and my three children. It was always on the grow! And today that love has grown to include a wonderful son-in-law and even to his two brothers who feel like sons to me too one of which even asked his mom if he was supposed to call me "mom" too now since we were all 'related' by marriage! I was so touched!

Multiplying your love, in my experience as a mom, has brought thousands of joys in my life. It has also brought tons of worry, anxiety, and sorrow too. Like when my freshly married daughter followed her husband two thousand miles away in his new job. How would I, the mom who had to hold everyone's hand in at the mall, who didn't go to sleep at night until I had looked in and blessed all of my kids and knew they were safely at home, who uses text messaging as a crutch to check in on my kids who aren't living at home any more, deal with a child moving that far away? And then not only the miles, but the two hour time difference. I was going to bed when she was getting off work! Multiply the love, says the Holy Spirit.

Who knew multiplying the love would help in mileage too? Not me and if you would have tried to sell me on that before they moved, there would have been No Sale! I still don't like it, but since I haven't won the lottery and can pay them to stay local, I guess I have to be thankful they have jobs and are experiencing the closeness and bonding of a married couple only being so far apart from family can do.

Multiplying the love helps me get through the day after my son tells me he is planning a trip to go sky diving, or my other daughter joining a college group to travel to our nation's capitol to take part in a conference. Multiplying the love means I am able to deal with my husband's blood sugar drops and lows with diabetes and knowing what to do without panicking.

When this same sister-in-law was pregnant with her seventh child, she went into premature labor at 19 weeks. She was put on bed rest, then a hospital stay, but my tiny niece was born at 21 weeks, with a very slight chance of surviving.

There in the hospital, inside an incubator, with tubes and lines going all over her tiny little body which at the time didn't even have skin growing on it yet, I wondered how in the world my brother and his wife could cope with this when they had to leave her at the hospital and go home to their other six children who needed them too. Once again, the Holy Spirit shut me up and instead of my words, the Spirit's words opened my mouth to reassure them, "Her guardian angels will be here the whole time with her, I know they are here with her." Multiplying love. It works miracles and somehow they were able to go home, get rest and reassure their children everything was in the Lord's hands.

I take no credit for knowing anything about Multiplying Love. It's a phenomenon of the Holy Spirit. Truly. I only know that it is incredibly hard to do, make no mistake, it takes prayer, tons and tons of prayer. But you know where Multiplying Love comes from? Trust.

Trust: That word weighs like a ton. It settles on your shoulders and your heart. And the ONLY one you can trust with all the weight and the worries, anxieties, fears and sorrows is God. It's a constant work in progress, it is an action; trust. I wake up every day having to recommit to it. It does not come easily some days. Trusting in God and letting go of myself is like having to do exercise! But the more you do it, the better you get at it. I didn't say it becomes easier, because it does not. But you can manage it and get better at trusting and love. Trust is what fuels Multiplying Love. Multiplying Love comes directly from God. He is so very good at love and it's nothing for Him to love the billions of people in this world all the same at the same time.

So TRUST = MULTIPLYING LOVE

Your candle will not diminish, only grow all the brighter as you light the candle of others!

"When one door closes another door opens; but we so often look so long and so regretfully upon the closed door, that we do not see the ones which open for us."

~ Alexander Graham Bell
and Helen Keller

"You must do the thing you think you cannot do."

~ Eleanor Roosevelt

Yes, I needed two quotes this week to remind me that I can do this. Last week I wrote about being strong and facing those moments in parenting when you have to let go by multiplying love. Right?

Well, this week I am totally failing in that letting go thing. Laura, spoiler alert, your mom is still a control freak and I fail quite frequently!

Control, yes, those of us who think we are good at it have to have constant 2 x 4's slapped across our foreheads reminding us we are NOT in control. As much as we would like to think we can be, should be, that it is our God-given right to be, our good and gracious God keeps giving us lessons, I mean opportunities to let go and let Him do everything.

For all my bravado last week in talking about Multiplying Love, I am failing miserably in the mom department through three time zones this week. I am embarrassed to say that I have spent the last three nights unable to sleep because I'm worried about one daughter spending the week on one coast, taking a college course, and the other daughter on the other coast driving through rain storms. Now after 26 years of being a mom, I KNOW God is in charge, I KNOW my children are adults, and I KNOW I simply cannot tri-locate to be everywhere. However, in my heart, late at night, there is a part of me that still thinks I can. And when I can't, I worry. And when I worry, I don't sleep.

So now it's Wednesday and sleep deprived me is trying to work at my full time job in the church office, help teach at our family martial arts business because we are short handed this week, *and* still pretend that I am a fully functioning adult who won't burst into tears at any given moment because she wants all her children closer to home.

It's enough to send me over the edge wishing for life when my children were little and I worried about the fever one of them had.

"You must do the thing you think you cannot do." Eleanor says, yet letting your children grow up, watching your parents get old and be lonely when one of them passes, is harder than I would have ever imagined. It's during those nights, lying wide awake that I fear I will not be able to do this. Has any

mother died from worrying too much? Or is it just a cumulative thing, hence the gray hair, wrinkles, heart conditions, stomach ailments that wear our bodies down? Why is it we can be so very good at letting God take care of things one moment and the next be right back worrying again in the next?

The human condition is constantly battling over this. We KNOW God loves us, and is in charge, yet we despair and worry, and think we can change things. That Mom power is so very powerful we can move mountains – literally!

Peace only comes when you become so worn out by crying, worn out from shaking your head at God saying "Come on, why can't it be MY way this time?" Worn out from sheer exhaustion of willpower that still does not change anything because, guess what, that's life. It is NOT perfect, or just the way you want it. No matter HOW HARD YOU THINK YOU CAN CHANGE THINGS.

I come from warrior women stock. My people descended from the nomadic Germanic tribes that came from the frozen north, invaded the Romans, and built a country or two. We sailed ships to coming to America looking for a better life for our children. We did those things. But in the end, we still cannot control everything.

Peace comes only when resignation, not in the sense of defeat, but in the acquiescence of our will to God's will finally settles lightly upon our souls. It isn't like a hammer, it doesn't come suddenly. It floats down upon us like a feather, and like a balm, spreads the ointment of "just let it be."

I keep thinking, okay, I get it. But as time goes on, I realize you never "get it" all the time. It's a constant learning thing. Uggg...grow tired of lessons. I grow tired of growing... I read the Psalms in the Bible and I begin to understand that it's not just me...it's all of mankind...having to be molded and shaped...because it will never be MY will to be done...molded and shaped, fired and beaten, into tensile steel of love...multiplying love that will always win out in the end because God made me this way. He made me strong, and controlling. He made me a wife, mother, daughter, sister and friend and in becoming great at all those things takes time, tears, patience and love. And the greatest of these is love.

Lent...Again...

Am I the only one not looking forward to Lent? I have to admit working in a church office, it seems like Lent happens a lot. I know it's only once a year. Perhaps it's because I am surrounded by well meaning publishers pushing whatever books, leaflets, bulletin blurbs they have available for us to use during Lent, or it's the retreats, workshops, and many, many more suggestions for Lent to make available to parish members that we advertise in our bulletin, hall and website that are making me weary.

I feel like a complete Catholic failure when by the time I get to Lent I am exhausted with the idea of "doing" Lent! Shame on me, I know. I think I stated once before I feel like the 'black sheep' of the office staff because sometimes I don't 'get it' with everything Catholic all the time.

So forgive my weariness. I am reminded that Jesus, too, grew weary with his Lent, His Passion of the Cross. He fell down three times. I know I fall a lot more, but I always know I can count on the fact that He did it too to help me get back up and face whatever sorrow, hurt or depression that is going on in my life.

So don't get me wrong with I say I really dislike Lent. Because I LOVE Holy Week. Which may sound weird, but I love the readings, the walking with Jesus through the Garden, admonishing his friends to stay awake and watch out for temptations.

I don't enjoy fasting on Friday, but I love Good Friday service. There is a song my sister-in-law and I do almost every year on Good Friday. It is called "The Pieta" and is written by Tom Kendzia. It is Mary's Song of the Crucifixion. It's hauntingly soft theme is about Mary asking us to come with her and see what our sin has done to her Son, the Lamb of God. It is so beautiful that every year it is hard for me to sing, because as a mom I envision myself standing there in front of my dying son. It reminds me again of Jesus love for us and Mary's love too because she once again says, 'yes' to Jesus. She didn't scream and holler, she accepted what Jesus accepted. As a mom I cannot imagine not yelling at the soldiers, doing something to make them stop. But Mary knew in her heart that what Jesus was doing, He had to do. It's a powerful thing to realize she knew He had to die. What beautiful faith Mary has in her son. And what strength she had to have to wait there, watching, praying, loving her son.

So maybe this Lent I can keep that in mind and realize that all of Lent is preparing for that moment of Jesus on the Cross and knowing I too have to say 'yes' to the sacrifices, and offerings up we try to do because Jesus died for me and for you. And He chose to do it.

Tang of Living

Jack London, author of Call of the Wild and White Fang, referred to his life as his "adventure path" and was always in pursuit of the "tang of living."

Aren't we, as Catholics called to the "tang of living?" What is faith all about if it doesn't give a flavor to our lives? If we don't use faith to help us move mountains, follow our dreams and live the life God gave us with zeal and enthusiasm?

Sometimes we get bogged down in everything bad going on, wars, fights, battles for morality. We tend to forget our "tang for living."

Today I will seek my "tang" or the zest in life, and not forget that life is about the enthusiasm of living!

"Joy is the serious business of heaven." C.S. Lewis

Easter

Holy Week already here

Mass of Chrism male voices appear

Feet washed clean on Thursday night

Good Friday Passion gives my heart fright

Holy Saturday no longer sin slaves

Happy Easter! Alleluia !Christ is Risen from the grave!

April

"I cried aloud to the LORD, and he answered me from his holy hill. Selah"

~ David, King of Israel

Yesterday, while leading a Communion Service with some of the students of our parish grade school, I had a most embarrassing moment. At least from my point of view it was. I was proclaiming the gospel, the one where Mary Magdalene had come to the tomb and could not find Jesus. Then when she turned, she saw two angels and there stood Jesus. But she didn't recognize Him until He spoke her name. While reading the part where she recognized him, I began crying.

I cannot explain why this happened except I was so caught up in the thought of losing Jesus then finding Him again that I broke into tears.

While I was hoping the students and adults sitting in the pews would think I had just lost my voice for a moment from the same allergies plaguing all of us this season, it wasn't until today, while reading an article on Catholic News Agency that I know what happened.

Pope Francis, during his short homily on the very same gospel I read that day, was telling the faithful to "Pray for the gift of tears" to see the Risen Christ, just like Mary Magdalene.

Suddenly I began crying again. I should not have been embarrassed when that happened to me yesterday; I had received a gift from Jesus! I was awestruck. It's one of those moments you want to shout to everyone around you, "Oh my gosh, listen to this! This happened to me!" And yet, even though I work in a parish office, I felt funny calling attention to myself about this, it felt self centered. So while I write this to you in this blog, I'll figure out how to inform my office mates because I don't want to hide a God moment from anyone. Like miracles, we need to share God moments in our lives to help each other on our faith journeys. Thanks for sharing in my God moment!

"Risk more than others think is safe. Care more than others think is wise. Dream more than others think is practical. Expect more than others think is possible. "

~ Cadet Maxim

...and be defiantly thankful! Yes, thankful for the adversity in your life, when others put you down because you stick up for your moral values, be grateful for their taunting. When others ask you to join in something you know is not right, and you refuse, be grateful for the test.

For without adversity we learn nothing. Without testing, we fail. Without questions, faltering, or temptations we are falsely lead to thinking life is easy. We get spoiled. Then something comes along and knocks us flat on our behinds.

When I was in my twenties and thirties I thought if you just lived as you ought, everything should work out, be okay. If you are sick, you get well; if you get hurt it won't be a lot. Now in my fifties, I finally see life is not about avoiding all those things. It's about building your faith to the point that WHEN those things happen you will trust in God to see you through it.

Jesus was tempted by the devil to give up all his suffering and enjoy a kingdom here on earth. We too are tempted by the devil to the very same thing. Give up moral values, live temporary in this life and get all your want. Whether it's greed, all the sex we want with whomever, all the drug taking, fast life choices, and never, ever paying any gratitude to the one Creator who put us here.

But Jesus didn't take that bribe. Jesus, while carrying a hundred pound cross, fell three times. He was God, why did He fall? Why didn't angels just hold that up for him? Could it be He was showing us how to get up every time we fall? That's we can always look to God to help us when we fall?

While getting lashed with nasty bone crushing whips, Jesus hung on, didn't die on the spot, but waited for more horrors lashed on the cross to die, he didn't give up until it was time, until he knew he had finished His mission on earth; to offer himself up as a sacrifice for sin.

How can we hear the story of Jesus and not think of what he did for us? How can WE not do more for others, for ourselves, by living a moral, value filled life after what He did? We don't want to be made fun of, yet He was. We don't want to suffer, yet He did. And it was all for us, not one iota was for himself.

People made fun of him for risking more than what was safe, for caring more than others thought wise, for dreaming of His Father in heaven who knew and loved Him. And Jesus left behind 11 apostles whom He expected to carry on His Father's church on earth and even expected Peter, who had denied Him three times, the power to get people to heaven.

Risk more than others think safe, care more than others think wise, dream more than others think practical and expect more, both out of others and out of ourselves because, my friend, we are on a journey that does not end in this life. It's not all about what I want in life. It's about looking forward to a better place where all the trials are gone and life goes on forever!

Arise!

In the gospel, "Maid! Arise" is "Talitha Cumi," which is Aramaic. How did this little bit of Aramaic get itself embedded in the Greek of the gospels? There can be only one reason.

Mark got his information from Peter. For the most part, outside of Palestine at least, Peter, too, would have to speak in Greek. But Peter had been there; he was one of the chosen three, the inner circle, who had seen this happen.

And he could never forget Jesus' voice. In his mind and memory he could hear that "Talitha Cumi" all his life. The love, the gentleness, the caress of it lingered with him forever, so much so that he was unable to think of it in Greek at all, because his memory could hear it only in the voice of Jesus and in the very words that Jesus spoke.

The Gospel of Mark
(The Daily Bible Series, rev. ed.)

"When it is dark enough, you can see the stars."

~ Ralph Waldo Emerson

I found this quote especially applicable this week as we seem to be hearing about one tragedy after another in our country. It's hard to write about encouraging words without sounding trite at times like these, but we really do have to remember that God is always with us during these times. And to remember that it isn't God that brings on these tragedies, sin and the choice of Adam and Eve for us to have to live with the consequences of sin is what makes mankind's behavior so awful at times.

But God did promise that He would be by our sides during these times and we can see His work among the hundreds of good people who help those hurt or injured and among the prayers that so many of us are pouring upon all those victims in these tragedies. Please keep praying for our country.

Don't wait for a light to appear at the end of the tunnel, run down there and light the bloody thing yourself!

-anonymous

Time for a new week, time for more positive happy news. Okay guys bring it on in. Cricket.....cricket...

Another week of finding my own happiness to talk about, huh? Are you feeling like that lately? With all the bad things in the news and the news media only talking about the bad things you begin to feel the world is horrible. Well, sometimes it is, but really for the most part people are trying to be good and are helping other people.

My quote this week focuses on doing...not waiting for others or the news media to report on it, but doing good ourselves, being the light at the end of the tunnel. If we get nothing out of the events of the past week it should be, look at all of the people who rushed in to help those injured people! And they weren't just First Responders although each of those people deserves a medal! But other people helped too. Why aren't their names in the news? Why do we even NAME the people who commit these terrible things?

Let's begin looking at the good in people, the people who go exploring down dark places and remember to bring a candle, match or flashlight so they can illuminate the way for those following! Are we like them?

To be a leader these days means having a lot of courage. It takes guts to not only stand up and run into a burning building, a place where bombs could go off, but also to know your values and morals and not be afraid of being make fun of for speaking up or against things that go against those values. To not be afraid of being considered a "judgmental" person or a non-tolerant person because we believe in certain morals truths.

That light at the end of the tunnel, the one we help light is there to lead people on the straight and narrow way, not the lemmings falling to their deaths in the sea of moral waste!

That tunnel in the quote reminds me of a long, unending tunnel I biked through several years ago while on a 'rails to trails' path in Southern Illinois.

My family loves to bike and about twelve years ago we packed up the bikes and headed to the Vienna, Illinois bike trail, an old railroad line that had been turned into a walking and biking trail. It's about nine miles long and it goes through absolutely beautiful country, meadows, woodlands, and crosses bridges with waterfalls and rivers. It is gorgeous! At the northern end of the trail is a tunnel. A very long old train tunnel which, if you were traveling by train, you would get through much more quickly than walking or riding a bike.

This tunnel had no lights; you went into it like many railroad tunnels where the hill begins to rise up on the sides so there are rocks or timbers holding in the hill as you head toward the entrance of the tunnel. It almost looks like you've entered the point of no return. Once you entered the tunnel, there was a point of no return because it was so completely dark inside you had to keep going forward toward that teeny speck of light, the opening on the other end because if you risked stopping inside the tunnel a myriad of things might happen to you, there were bats overhead and you felt them swooping over your head, the gravel over which your bike tires crunched was a little thicker inside and tended to grab at the rubber throwing you off balance so going forward was the only thing keeping you upright. You realize that you are in a point of no return because claustrophobia sets in and the only way to keep from hyperventilating is to not stop!

Not all tunnels have lights at the end of them, not all lights at the end of the tunnel will illuminate your way, but sometimes if you are stuck in a tunnel you may have to keep going and light the way for yourself and others. It may not be a tunnel you want to go down, kind of like paths in life. We are forced into certain situations whether of our own making of someone else's but we find ourselves having to be the ones to help get us and everyone else out. Keeping our heads and trusting God to guide us is the only way to keep going forward, keep speaking out, keeping being the moral truth-teller in this world and to help celebrate the other people who rush in to bad situations to help! I want to be that person who helps!

Life is not about waiting for the storms to pass... It's about learning how to dance in the rain.

- Vivian Greene

Ain't that the truth, Sister?! If it's not one thing it's another. You could go on and on with all the little sayings in life, but one thing is sure, we are always trying to get through all the little and big obstacles in life and there are LOTS of them at times. Hence the Encouraging Words!

Dancing in the rain seems to be the norm these days. I'm sure it's because I'm getting, ahem... a little older and know about more things than when I was a carefree kid just glad it was finally warm and sunny outside! My hubs and I have decided that what makes us crabby as adults is the wear and tear on us as we have navigated so many years into middle age and have weathered several storms already. In our humanness we are bound to get a little weary and worn from those storms.

But maybe the whole point of getting older is a test to see just how long you can go in life without caving into crabbiness! I mean this whole blog is about being Young, Fun and Catholic! I personally think it's my Catholic faith which helps keep me young and fun and not wanting to give up on hope and trust in the Lord to see us through all the rain.

And rain is good, it waters our souls, it gives us things to be grateful for, because without the trials in life we wouldn't know we had it so good as kids! It's the looking back that makes you realize how blessed you have been, lucky and full of God's love. Sometimes when you are standing in the middle of the rain storm you realize that life is about rain storms, there are many and sometimes they are flooding, but you can always count on faith to help you paddle about.

My family has a funny story about weathering the pouring rain. About ten years ago we were putting an addition onto our house. During the construction process they had to tear off part of the roof to connect it to the new roof. With the rafters in place all they had to do was lay down the plywood and shingle it. But along came a great black cloud and to this day I honestly don't know what the workers were thinking aside from, "Let's get off this roof from the lightning" because they left our house without any protection from the approaching storm, it was open to the rain without a tarp, without the plywood or anything to keep the rain from getting inside.

My husband happened to come home for a late lunch at that moment and it was a good thing too because the skies had opened up and it began pouring, right into our kitchen, our bedroom and in the basement which was carpeted.

I was working as a school secretary at the time and he called me, I grabbed our kids and raced home to help bail water. The kids got basement duty and my hubs and I struggled in the ensuing storm to nail plastic tarps in place over the openings in the roof. I have never been so drenched in my life. It was raining so hard it was washing the contact lenses out of my eyes! My hubs was on a ladder in a shirt, dress slacks, tie and his good shoes nailing down plastic. When we finished that there was so much water on the open subfloor he had to drill holes into the wood to let it drain out.

The kids were grabbing towels sopping up water and putting them through the dryer to use again. It was a family effort! Afterwards we had some ruined wood flooring in the kitchen, a wet carpet in the basement and a few choice words for the contractor.

Now as we look back it's funny, but it surely was not a laughing matter when our entire house was at risk of flooding. But we learned a lesson that day and ever since keep a handy supply of tarp around in case anything needs covering before a rainstorm.

It's those lessons we learn in life about weathering storms, usually not quite so literally, that help us learn trust and keep us moving forward. If you can dance in the rain, you will come out of it okay. And the help of family and friends most certainly is important. And my Catholic faith teaches me that no matter what happens God is there with you. Because of original sin bad stuff happens, but God is still there to bail you out!

So don't get old and crabby! You can't stop aging, or bad things happening in life, but you CAN change your attitude about all that stuff! If you can dance in the rain, you can suffer through the storms knowing heaven is still in front of us, waiting to makes us happy!

May

"I may be compelled to face danger, but never fear it, and while our soldiers can stand and fight, I can stand and feed and nurse them."

~ Clara Barton, Founder of the American Red Cross

I thought of this yesterday after a conversation I had at a local store. I had overheard a conversation while standing in line between the checker and another customer. They were discussing the customer's son who was being deployed to Afghanistan next week. After he left the store the checker apologized to me for the wait and told me they went to church together and the situation.

My heart went out to both of them, the checker because she knew the family and had watched the son grow up, many times he had sat next to her in church and then to the dad who was trying to be very brave and tell the friend about his wife who was not bearing the news very well. After all, her son was deploying two days after Mother's Day.

I looked at her, my heart was hurting for all of them and I said hesitantly because I didn't really know her, "I will keep him in my prayers." And she looked up with the most beautiful smile and said, "Oh, I will too, in fact," she whispered, "I keep a list on my refrigerator of people to pray for."

Wow, that's beautiful! I thought, here we were sharing this information as strangers yet there was a connection of prayer, people needing other people. We are all called to pray for each other!

I may not be able to change the world, or make things as they once were, but I can tell people I am praying for them and it makes a difference! I may not be fighting a war, not a physical one, but I am joining in the spiritual fight to unite people everywhere in praying for others, and knowing God is watching over us all.

What memories smells bring us. My sense of smell is at times a curse, when I can smell milk gone bad in the fridge before you even open the door, or something overly ripe in the grocery. But there are other times my sense of smell has reminded me of the delights of childhood. Like today, my hubs, youngest daughter and I were on our town's bike trail. I love this 7 mile blacktop trail that winds from the north end of town, through suburbs, retail sites, county park, baseball diamonds, soccer fields to the south end of town. You would think it was totally insane that you could do that in a matter of an hour, but on a bike and the way the trail follows one of the many creeks that drain rain and creek water towards the Mississippi, you get to enjoy the sites, sounds and today especially, the smells.

Honeysuckle plants are the most delicious smelling flower on earth. I know they are weeks, invasive, once getting a hold of anything in your yard they are like the march of the locusts. But honeysuckle is one of those smells you remember as a child and that aroma stays with you. It's comfort from summer nights, hearing crickets, being hugged by your mom or dad or grandparent. It's sitting on porch swings watching heat lightning in the distance and hearing the frogs croak their hellos to each others. Songs are written about this week. Why? Because it invokes such memories in all of us.

The other wafting aroma we enjoyed along the way today, was barbeque. Specifically, because we live in southeast Missouri which is close enough to St. Louis, barbeque pork steaks, slathered in sauce, cooked on a charcoal grill. It was enough to make me want to dump my bike, wade over the creek and make a new friend! "Hi there! I was passing by on my bike, along the trail and could not miss the awesome aroma of your lunch on the grill! Mind if I stay?"

My dad was one of the best griller of all times, alongside my husband! He never did anything fancy, it was hamburgers, or hotdogs, brats or pork steaks. That was pretty much his fare. No chicken, no fancy steaks. But anything he grilled he slathered with sauce, Kraft Original recipe that is. In fact, when I got married, I insisted my husband learn how to grill just like my dad.

As my dad got older, he could still dish up a mean grill, but usually my hubs or my brother were out there "helping" because he would leave the meat on a tad too long. But he never left off the sauce. Ummmm.....deep basted Kraft Original recipe sauce, cooked on until it's almost black, is the best tasting burgers or pork you've ever had!

Memories live on in our sense of smell. Think about it.

June

Thoughts on today: saw a momma and daddy robin coaxing baby bird out from the bushes to fly. How hard they have to work to convince baby that it's okay, it's what they have to do to grow up. Much like human parents showing their kids the world, how to drive, how to make a living. How hard it is for parents to do their part. After all that work, you're sad they have flown away, yet you know it's your job to do!

Last week was full of a lot of anxiety in our household, job anxiety. Once again God showed us He was in charge. Yet He never tips His hand to show us what is next. "Trust." He just keeps saying, "Trust."

I never realized how very hard it is to trust the Lord in matters so important like raising kids, getting/keeping a job or where the next one is leading you, and just living your life.

Even in my 50's now it's still hard for me to just "trust" and not think I have to physically (mentally, emotionally, etc.) move my own mountains or figure things out.

As I write, my hubs is having to trust the Lord in a job interview that should have been his five years ago. Why does the Lord make us wait so long for things we work so hard on sometimes? Why does it seem like everyone else gets the breaks, the miracles, the prayers answered?

I'm reminded of that saying, "Ours is not to question why, ours is just to do and die." I know it's from a war movie or general or something, but it seems like life is like that and God asks that of us. Don't question it, just do it and I'll come through."

So, okay Lord, whatever you say.

Oh, and that quote is from the poem, "Charge of the Light Brigade" by Alfred, Lord Tennyson.

Charge of the Light Brigade

Say it with Love

Listening to the Moody Blues and their song, "Say It With Love" and that is an excellent way to live your life. No matter what, say things with love.

That is totally what Jesus told us to do. Love your neighbor as yourself. Love God best of all. Love your neighbor. Despite our differences, our emotions, if we could just remember to say things with love, even when we are upset and mad about something.

And has it been a good year to try to say things with love! No matter where you turn these days there is controversy. And yet we are still called to correct our neighbor, point out the truth in all matters. But we can do it with love. I don't recall hearing Jesus screaming at anyone about their sins. He said everything with love, especially when pointing out their faults and failings.

Would it not be the coolest thing if our entire world could accept everyone is different, and help each other by saying things with love? It doesn't mean we accept their sins, but we can help correct them with brotherly love.

Say it with love today!

July

This week I am focusing on fun. My dad had a way of using little sayings that always cracked me up. I don't know where he came up with these things, if he read them somewhere which could be very true because he read books like crazy. But it was fascinating listening to them. Things like, "Well, you're cuter than a little spotted pup trotting beneath a red wagon!" or "They are slower than a herd of turtles stampeding through peanut butter."

He always made me laugh with these so I found some to share with you too!

1. I love deadlines. I especially like the whooshing sounds they make as they fly by!

2. Someday we'll look back on all this and run into a parked car.

3. Tell me what you need and I'll tell you how to get along without it!

4. I hate when my Reality Check bounces.

5. When everything is coming your way, you're in the wrong lane.

6. I used to have an open mind but my brains kept falling out.

7. Everybody is somebody else's weirdo.

8. Everyone has a photographic memory. Some just don't have film.

9. I poured Spot remover all over my dog. Now he's gone.

10. Just remember, you are absolutely unique. Just like everyone else.

"Change pushes us to get out of ourselves and rely on God."

Abe Lincoln once said that people are about as happy as they make up their minds to be. And you know, it's true, happiness doesn't just happen. Sometimes you have to really work at it. Sometimes, you just have to make up your mind, make a decision or a choice to be happy because life doesn't always play fair, give you all the right cards or go your way all the time.

We just got back from traveling almost 2,000 miles to see daughter, Laura and her hubs. As I was putting away the five loads of laundry that awesome daughter, Cait, did while I headed right back to work, I thought about how much the change in our lives can affect our moods.

I miss having her closer, being able to visit physically more often because I am a homebody and I like to have my family close, but if I mope around wishing she was closer to home, what good does that do her or me?

Instead I need to be thankful we had the most wonderful time visiting them. We lived adventures while we were out there, going to the ocean, hiking up mountains, playing frenetic outdoor laser tag and those things should all be foremost in my mind.

The same thing goes for our other two kids. They are growing up, meeting new people, finding jobs or going to schools that may lead them not so nearby either but that is change. Change can be good if we can look at that way. Change can mean fun, happiness, adventure, memories to make, stories to tell. Change pushes us to get out of ourselves and rely on God.

It seems to be a tendency for us humans to see the sad, bad or gloomy especially when things change. When family members or friends die, when someone becomes very ill or we lose a job or a child moves out of the house. Sad change really takes work, a lot of work. There's no getting around the fact that losing someone is a huge mood changer.

When I read about saints it seems they were always extolled for their ability to be happy during bad times or the way they could bring good out of bad. I'm not very good at that yet. Change sometimes makes me sad and wish for other days, long ago days or better times.

But change forces us to choose. Sometimes I don't choose well. While I don't always have control over body chemistry, illness or injury, I can choose to deal with it with a good attitude and even then when I fail I know that at least trying is what counts.

I encourage you to choose to try to think of change as a positive challenge, even if it is not happy or is painful. It begins with you. Let's rise to the challenge together!

July

"...I have heard people rant and rave and bellow
That we're done and we might as well be dead,
But I'm only a cockeyed optimist
And I can't get it into my head."

I woke up with this song from "South Pacific" in my head today. I don't know if it's because it was Monday or if I'm just tired of all the pessimistic news all the time. I like keeping up on the world and what's going on, but why does it seem like it's always bad news all the time? So when this song broke into my head first thing I thought I'd go with that attitude this morning at least for as long as I could!

Cockeyed optimist sees the world in a different way. Granted they may not always be happy or optimistic, but just as a way of life try to look at the sunnier sides of things. Like the silly mother rabbit who decided to have her babies in a very shallow depression in the middle of our fenced in yard. Smack in the middle of dog country. We thankfully discovered the newborns before the dog did and moved them outside of the fence. Our poor spaniel, in which is bred the instincts of hunting exactly such little creatures is going nuts. He knows exactly where we moved that nest and he keep trying to dig and chew his way through the fence to get at them. He just wants to play... but his way of playing with our nine year Siamese cat inside the house is to grab her head and wrestle. Luckily for our cat, she goes along with him until he gets too rough and cuffs him one in the nose when he pulls too hard. Somehow I don't think baby bunnies would have that kind of resilience. So we moved the nest.

Next, in an obvious effort to keep our poor dog entertained, Mother Nature told a momma cat to have her new litter under our deck. So now we have new bunnies AND new kittens all over the place. Cockeyed optimists that we are we just keep telling the dog to stop chewing the boards, move whatever bunnies and kittens that escape from their safe homes into the dog's part of yard and try to appreciate all the new life that is apparently finding our yard a nice "home".

Isn't that what cockeyed optimism does though? It takes something seemingly silly or unimportant and makes it seem like the right thing to do. While others may scoff at our Pollyanna point of view, it helps us to view the world with good cheer and hope. Because what is optimism? It's hope. Hope in the future; hope that things will get better or that we can deal with it if it doesn't. Optimism tells us that we have a reason to get up in the morning and most importantly that God is in charge.

Why does God put two seemingly diverse creatures together in the same yard? He knows the dog is going to go after the bunnies. Is it an opportunity for my family to feel like we are having a positive impact on the world that in some small way we are "coming to the rescue" of small innocents? So when we read about the horrible things people do to one another we feel we are in some small way trying to make the world a better place even just in our own yard? It could be the lesson too that even if we try our best, bad things may happen? The dog may yet act on his instincts and hurt another creature and we just have to live with the consequences also known as the circle of life.

Creatures and people are born and die. Yet they all have meaning especially to God. We may not know their purpose, but He does. Doesn't that make being an optimist, cockeyed or otherwise, a good thing?

I believe it does...

"...I could say life is just a bowl of Jello
And appear more intelligent and smart,
But I'm stuck like a dope
With a thing called hope,
And I can't get it out of my heart!
Not this heart"

On Being A Writer: Louis de Wohl (1903-1961)

WHEN A MAN HAS REACHED A CERTAIN AMOUNT OF SUCCESS in his profession, people will come to him and ask questions. Now whenever someone asked me "Should I become a writer?" I invariably answered point-blank "No." Some were hurt, some angry, almost all of them were surprised. "Why not?" "Because you haven't got the stuff in you." "How do you know? You have never read anything I have done, have you?" "No. But I know all the same. I know because you asked me. If you had the stuff in you that makes a writer, you wouldn't ask me, you'd go and write and go on writing. You couldn't abstain from it."

And that goes, in my opinion, for all creative work; for would-be actors, architects, painters, sculptors, and musicians. Mind you, there are quite a number of people who cannot abstain from it, although they do not have the stuff in them, but that is beside the point.

As for me, I started writing at the age of seven or just a little older, and what really set me off was that some of the stories I read did not go the way I wanted. I simply decided to change them, and change them I did. At the age of eight I wrote a play, "Jesus of Nazareth," and the great speech of the High Priest Caiphas in the marketplace of Jerusalem bore a strong resemblance to Mark Antony's speech in Shakespeare's Julius Caesar. Caiphas praised Christ in the same hypocritical way that Mark Antony praised Brutus, to convince his audience of the contrary.

Plagiarism or not, I was very much in earnest about my drama. I decided to compose the music for it myself, paint the posters and design the scenery, and of course I myself would play one of the leading parts, Caiphas perhaps, or Mary Magdalene

I laughed out loud when I read the part of Louis de Wohl's biography where he writes that some of the stories he read when he was 7 years old did not "go the way I wanted. I simply decided to change them and change them I did."

I did the same thing when I was about the same age! I had a mystery book which characters included two boys and a girls all the same age. I changed their names to my own and two friends and changed some of the adventures they had to match my own. From there I decided I could write my own stories and began my career as a budding writer by age 8!

And what he said about knowing if someone is a writer or not? I understood his somewhat cut to the quick answer too. Too many times I've had people tell me, wow that's so great you have written a book. I've always wished I could write a book!" And I look at them and say, "Well, why haven't you?" And they stumble around with this excuse or that. But really, what is your excuse for not writing a book? I self published all my books so you can't use the, "No body will look, buy, read, care, or whatever, my book." That is no excuse! I didn't care if anybody read my stories. I liked them, I wrote them for my own enjoyment. It was just a fluke that my kids like to read them too and some other kids and some friends. I didn't begin trying to write for all of them, just me!

So if you ARE a writer, first of all you already know you are so you don't need to ask me or anyone else and secondly, get writing. Buy notebooks and begin...there is no excuse!

Peace

Please, please, please, let there be peace on earth and if only it could begin with me. I have a fellow blogger who lives in Lebanon and she is worried for her family's safety. She has little babies, she has fellow countrymen.

Please continue to pray for our world and for the world peace that still seems to elude us.

God please hear the prayers of the few who listen to you, make us strong and have voices to spread your Word and your peace.

September

Smile!

Have you ever noticed that there are days you need to live life light? Those days when you aren't feeling your best, other people are getting on your nerves, when you feel like the world is becoming a much more scary place?

Live life light on those days and smile.

Living life light means bring your thoughts to a happy level, don't think so deeply on things. My mom used to admonish me when she noticed I was sitting at the kitchen table or on the couch with a pensive look on my face. "You're thinking too deeply about something," she would warn. In other words, stop worrying about whatever you are worrying about! And she was almost always right. I was worrying about something.

Living life light doesn't mean you don't care about life or don't take anything seriously. But honestly, there are days when we just need to sit at the stoplight and stop being mad at the bad drivers, maybe us included, stop being mad at the world for raising tyrants and ego maniacs. We need to remember that God is in charge of everything. We can pray and ask for help, but wringing our hands, worrying and moaning and groaning won't get Him to listen to us any more than having a cheerful smile and saying, "Okay, you got this, Lord."

So try it. Sit there and smile. Come on. Think of puppies running over that little kid on that soda commercial, think of Bill Crosby saying "JELLO".

When I'm thinking too deeply I remember the video of me tripping down the steps at my sister's wedding! Or how the bears I knit make me smile. Or the joy on the face of that little kid down the street trying out a new bike the day after Christmas.

Begin a list: Smile list:

I got that Joy, joy, joy, joy, down in my heart, down in my heart, down in my heart to stay!"

At first the Pope scared me last week with his message of de-emphasizing the top "hot" buttons the Church has right now, abortion, gay marriages, the Healthcare debates. It was after talking with my wonderful husband, (thank you, Michael) that he pointed out maybe Pope Francis is trying to get us all back to what our Catholic faith is about, **Joy and Hope.**

Yes, all of those other things are important to keep fighting for, but if in the fight we lose sight of the Joy of our Catholic faith and the Hope that our faith can give us, then we might as well have lost the battle.

What makes our Catholic Faith different from all other faiths? Besides the fact that it is the one that can trace its roots directly to Christ, for two thousand years it has been the faith of joy and hope to people who were down trodden, slave, sick, disheartened, poor and lonely. The Pope is calling us to live in Joy and Hope, not fear of what the world can do to us, not fear of what tomorrow might bring because we don't know if tomorrow will come. We need to live in the joy and hope of our faith this very day.

Jesus admonished the adulterous woman by simply saying to her, "Go and sin no more," yet he condemned those people who were slanderous, telling them they are murdering their fellow men in their hearts when they hate and gossip. Ouch, how many times have I slung oaths and curses at people simply because they get in my way or argue with me? Are we no better than the Sadducees and Pharisees when we get angry and yell at those people who disagree with the Church's teachings? Aren't we called to love? Yes, we do not condone, but to let anger rule our faith life is no way to **live** our faith life.

Satan plays on our righteous indignation; he knows exactly how to pull us out of our joyful, hopeful, peaceful selves by taunting us with occasions to get mad at the world and the events that unfold. It is any different of a world than it was 2,000 years ago? People did evil things then too, but Jesus didn't let that rock his boat and told his apostles to stay calm in the midst of the stormy seas.

Our seas are pretty stormy now too, and I've slipped under the surface of the water trying to get to Jesus plenty of times. Like Peter, Jesus has had to stretch out his hand to me and say, okay, Lisa of little faith, I've gotten my Church through this before, I won't abandon you now. Stop being angry, stop hurting with your words and thoughts!

So let's get our joyful back on and show the devil he can't defeat us. We have God on our side!

My family is often amused at my frequent use of the term, "**Just, offer it up.**" IT meaning whatever it is that is bothering them, real pain, sadness, lack of something they see as a necessity but really isn't food, water or shelter, or even some person who is deemed as being a 'pain in the neck."

But no matter how hard I try, nor how old my kids and my loving hubs is, I still feel it necessary to instill good values into them, hence why I use this term so much. My own mother still tells ME to "Offer it up!" so why should be own family be exempt?

Offering it up, is a way for us to share in Christ's suffering and I read a very good explanation of it today on one of my fav bloggers, HappyCatholic.

She shares, " Offering it up" helps us not to"waste the pain!" of whatever it is we are going through, whether it's a bad time, sadness or even an unpleasant medical procedure.

Offering it up essentially means, let's remember what Jesus went through, agony in the garden, the way of the cross and the extreme pain of the dying on the cross.

I once read someone comment on Jesus' suffering that they didn't think it was so much. This person thought Jesus didn't live in extreme poverty, he had friends and parents. Surely that "short time" on the cross wasn't as bad as being a child in Africa dying of AIDS?

Wow, first I thought, how audace you would even write something like that, much less think it. Then I thought this poor guy never really got to experience Jesus' love for him. To think Jesus' sufferings weren't as great as a child's?

Our little bit of "offering up" a suffering of ours is of course nothing like Jesus' suffering. He hung on that cross, short of breath, dying by way of drowning from lack of air, knowing people did not believe in the things He came to share with them, knowing He had tried his very best, yet there were those people laughing at him, scorning him like a common criminal while he died there for their sins. They didn't even realize what he was doing for their souls. He died for the little child, dying of AIDS because He knew HE was opening up heaven for that child!

So, next time you have the opportunity to "Offer it up," remember, it's not just a trite little phrase we use lightly as Catholics or Christians. We offer things up because we DO appreciate what Jesus did for us on the cross and it's a tiny way we can say thank you for his suffering, so WE could have eternal life!

Dance

May today be your day to dance lightly with life
to sing wild songs of adventure,
to invite rainbows and butterflies out to play,
to soar your spirit and unfurl your joy.
- Jonathan Lockwood Huie

This week we celebrate lives lived, of people who danced the short time they were on earth, who began families not knowing they would not get to live to see them grow all the way up, who embodied the spirit of faith and joy they were given the grace to share.

This week's reminder is to try to always spread joy in people's lives. You have no idea how you affect the people around you. It may be your smile, the pat on the back you gave or just doing a job with a happy heart that makes a difference in someone's life.

This week we buried two dads, both in their late 40's, both with young kids and tons of family and friends. Its times like these we have to work hard to remember that we need to live life to the fullest, with the grace God gives us, with joy and the hope of eternal life.

May God's peace be with them and their families and may their children feel their loving presence throughout their lives.

There is nothing better than the encouragement of a good friend.
- Katharine Butler Hathaway

Friends are so necessary in life. They build you up with encouraging words. This is a giant thank you to all my friends who believe in me, what I am doing in life whether it's in my home life or at my job. THANK YOU!

There is no passion to be found playing small - in settling for a life that is less than the one you are capable of living.
- Nelson Mandela

And then we need Encouraging Words to keep moving forward against the tide of negative thinking. So keep moving forward. I love that line from "Meet the Robinsons" don't you? It's so true of life. You must keep moving forward and not look back at the "what if's".

And to keep doing God's work, we must keep moving forward.

What are the worse words you can use in your church? "*We've never done it that way before!*"

What are some of the best words we can use? "**What can we do to be partners with God in mission?**

Autocorrect Isn't Always

Several years ago, my youngest daughter and I were traveling back from moving our oldest daughter into her new digs. My husband was working and so couldn't go along but he kept up with us by texting. Don't you just love texting? It comes in so handy letting family members know where you are, what you are doing and if you are okay?

Well, usually it does. In this case, my daughter was driving and my hubs had texted asking where we were, he was going to prepare supper for us when we arrived and was asking for our whereabouts. At the time I was still a little new at texting with a new smart phone. But it turns out it wasn't so very smart. I typed in "We passing through Festus." But the "smart" phone didn't recognize the town of Festus and for reasons still beyond my understanding to this day, changed my type into "We're passing through Death."

Well, you talk about getting a rise out of my husband! He immediately called me and asked what was going on!

So when society is telling us how to live and what is right and what is wrong, it's kind of like using Autocorrect on your phone. It's not always "smart" to listen to automatic society and it's suggestions. You need to follow your conscience and your morals!

Singing in the Line

I love music, and as my kids can well attest to, I am always making up music at home, in the car or, to their chagrin, while standing in a shopping line. Humming a ditty or making up words to music I hear helps me stay calm I tell them. It's better than knitting in line which I have threatened to do because one of my favorite knitting bloggers does that. It's better than saying nasty things about the wait time. So I hum while rocking back and forth holding my purchases.

This time of year trying to help spread a little extra patience and joy can make wipe you out. Honestly I don't have enough of my own to part with most days, but somehow just when you lease expect to have it, God zaps you with a little leftover patience to share; like sharing a giggle with the lady in line ahead of you over a child doing something funny in the next aisle.

I love the old Coke commercials where they use the song, "I'd like to teach the world to sing."

I wish every time I left the house, driving in my car, I would remember that song. I think it would help me calm down, be more patient and spread more joy to those around me.

Alas, still being the sinner I am, I don't always remember to do that.

But for today, driving in heavy "slit your wrist" traffic, I will endeavor to help teach the world to sing, one stoplight at a time!

Merry Christmas!

Daily Bread

Two hours before our Thanksgiving meal, I had my wonderful husband and my awesome youngest daughter working cleaning the house, when suddenly it came to me that dinner for our families would be much better if all shared at the same table as opposed to separate tables in two different rooms! Which meant, moving furniture.

Moving furniture is kind of a past time with me, it's in my DNA. My mom would move furniture every time my dad had to go out of town for meetings. It gave her something to do to pass the time until he was home again.

Anyway, 30 minutes later we had a new dining room; our old living room with the kitchen table in it along with a second table and chairs to go around. Move this dry sink here, a chair or two go downstairs and Ta-Da, a brand new Dining Room! Who needs a living room?

It worked so well that now, now, after New Year's we still have the room set up for dining where we eat every evening and don't even miss the living room. I love sitting at the table in a totally different atmosphere, with candles lit away from the middle of the kitchen. Though it's just the three of us most evenings, it's nice to catch up on the day eating soup, or meatloaf; the leftovers of Thanksgiving long gone, and enjoy the quiet of the new dining area. It's funny what a little change you make in your life can turn into a better habit, like going to Mass every day.

What began as just helping out at Mass because some of our Eucharistic Ministers were unable to be there all the time, has in two years time become a daily habit with me; serving the Lord by going to Mass, holding a Communion Service, training new altar servers or assisting our presiders during Mass. I don't think I could go back to sitting at my desk first thing in the morning. Now my day doesn't feel right, no matter how busy it's going to be, without going to Mass first.

I like change and I don't like change. Some change catches on and some doesn't. Unlike resolutions, change comes about out of necessities sometimes. Maybe that's the best way to change our prayer life too, out of a necessity of needing the Lord even more...sometimes on a daily bread!

Oh Mary Nagger of Jesus

Don't get me wrong, never would I EVER accuse the Blessed Mother of being anything but wonderful, holy and gentle...but it finally dawned on me the other night, as I lay in bed unable to sleep that I finally shared someting in common with our Blessed Mother. I struggle daily with not being a calm, gentle, quiet wife and mother, who looks constantly at Mary to be my example of how a wife and mother should me. I feel like I fail on every count. Mary said yes to God about having Jesus, even though she was very young, not married yet and was facing a stoning if anyone found out. She then rode on a donkey, nine months pregnant, had baby Jesus in a smelly stable, then when Joseph found out they could not return home for fear of Herod killing Jesus, she had to leave family and friends behind to make a new life in Nazareth.

Then Jesus gets lost while they are visiting the temple and makes no bones about it to her and Joseph when they ask why he disappeared. Never, ever, do we hear a complaint from Mary about all this? In fact we hear more about Joseph who was given dreams about what to do about all this. But Mary never says anything again after that, "yes," until the temple issue comes about.

It's not until Jesus is like 30 years old do we EVER hear that Mary said anything to Him. At a friend's wedding, when the couple runs out of wine, Mary, being a mom, and as all moms know, you find out these things, she found out about the wine trouble and went to Jesus. "Son, they are out of wine."

And quite surprisingly, at least to me, Jesus answers her back with, "Woman, that's really isn't my problem now, is it?"

But Mary had insisted or as I would label it now as "mom nagged" about it.

What joy! I lay in bed and pondered on this simple discovery. Mary had actually nagged her son about something. Although most historians and bible people don't list it like, I've seen the face and heard the sigh enough to recognize the words Jesus said to his mom that day, "Woman, my time has not yet arrived." It sounded to every bit to me like he was sighing and rolling his eyes at his mom. I know that sigh!!!

Having just come off a day of nagging our son who lives on his own, that he really needed to get a new car battery before the snow/cold Armageddon of 2014 hit the Midwest, or he'd be stuck at his job, late at night in the cold. My son, who can manage very well most of the time without interference from his mother, will on occasion stiffen up and refuse to budge when he feels Mom has gone a little overboard on the worry factor. I have finally come to warn him of impending text messages about the tornado that is headed our way, the holy day coming up, his sister from California is coming to town and he'd better make time to visit, or a multitude of other "mom" nags, into a "Obimom Alerts"

Obimom Alerts are text messages sent to any of my kids when I am worried about their welfare and I know they have plenty of common sense, but I still feel the need to warn, remind, or alert them to impending potential doom, illness or problems.

But now, I finally felt I knew Mary a little better. She had actually nagged her son to help someone! I felt like Ralphie in the *Christmas Story*, holding his Red Rider BB Gun as he fell asleep, smiling, content. It was okay to nag my kids on occasion, because Mary had done it!

Renovating Fun with the Picture Lady

I don't think I've mentioned the fact that our parish is in the midst of renovating our church. In the last five years, we've added a new building to our school complex, updated our rectory and this year it's time for the Church to get an "old" new look. This is all due to the generosity of our parish members who have donated both time, effort and money and to the wills and bequests of deceased members. God bless them all!

Since I began working in the parish office six years ago, I've had the pleasure of learning a lot about construction, change, moving furniture and taking pictures. The picture taking is the best part, I love seeing things in time lapse, what it looked like before and what it looks like now.

And that fascination has me browsing through our archives and finding old pictures taken inside the church. Wow, this is not the only renovation our 146 year old church has undergone. So rest assured, we are just keeping with our history of changing things, kind of like I am at home. Dining room? Hmm...we don't have one of those, let's make the living room into a dining room now...

Anyway, the picture taking, furniture moving etc. is not without it's pitfalls. Earlier this week Father and I were taking things down from the church attic; yes we have one of those, actually three of them if you count all the different spaces that exist in different parts of the church. He was standing up in the attic handing down some of our Christmas trees, I was standing on a cabinet taking things from him and dropping them to the floor, stood up and banged my head on the ceiling, not once but twice, then set down what I was carrying, stood up and did it again.

By this time our wonderful Pastor was in stitches laughing, although he did say God bless you afterwards, so I had that going for me. But it still hurt!

The next day we were moving cabinet drawers in the sacristy and I stepped back right onto a piece of molding with nails in it. Yep, you guessed it, I felt the slight pinch and my trusty tennis shoe was impaled with a nail. Luckily it didn't really pierce the skin on my foot, but I went directly to the Health Center for a tetanus shot!

It wouldn't be so funny, but this is like the third injury I've incurred while "helping" in Church since we've started renovating. It began when I tripped over the stairs in the choir loft when they were redoing the flooring there. It's never anything big, I just twisted my back and wore a heating pad for a week, but I'm beginning to get looks from the parish staff every time I go back and forth to Church. Lots of "be careful, Lisa!" follow me out the door.

While I am a self proclaimed klutz, after 30 years of teaching martial arts, I at least know how to fall correctly. But that training has yet help me avoid bumping my head, or watching what I step on.

My husband has threatened to send me to work in a hard hat, overalls and now heavy work boots to keep me safe.

I personally think my Guardian Angel is taking some much needed time off, but I do wish he'd get back from vacation, or quit taking a moment for himself! I mean I am working on God's work here, in His house. But I guess anytime you try to do something for the Lord, the devil is right there trying to trip you up, with me it's literal!

But I am getting some great pictures in the process! I have even received a nickname from the construction crew, and no it's not Klutz. I open the church door and walk and I hear, "Look out, it's the Picture Lady again!"

See, at least they have witnessed my embarrassing moments so far. I've luckily kept that only in front of Father and my family members, which is why I tell my husband I cannot possibly wear the hard hat and overalls in front of guys working inside church. It will be a dead give away that I'm a klutz in need of watching out for and get banned from taking more pictures.

I mean, there is scaffolding to scale, ladders to climb to get some really awesome shots of church, and the sanctuary...I can't ruin that!

It's like beating your head against a wall...

I truly wonder how God doesn't give up on us. I mean, time after time He must rescue us from our sins, forgive us and bless us. I imagine He must shake His head every time and say, "She still hasn't learned this lesson." sigh... "Let's try this again, Lisa!"

I say this because sometimes I don't learn my own lessons, the ones I try to teach to myself. For example, every week I must push an open cart carrying our Sunday bulletins in an open carton over to Church to be given out for the weekend. I've had this job now for over six years. I've carried them over in rain or shine, cold or heat. For the rain I cover the box with an umbrella or better yet a clean garbage bag. But there is something about windy days that does not sink into my graying head.

Windy days are the bane of my existence. I swear! I really dislike them. Now I love the breeze, I love the rising wind before a storm rolls in, the almost gale force breezes off the ocean while sitting on the beach. But a plain ole windy day in Southeast Missouri drives me to insanity.

This is especially true when it comes to carting my bulletins to the church. I think it has something to do with the subtle way Mother Nature does it. She thinks it's funny to watch me look out the door, see nothing going on weather wise and begin my journey down the ramp from the office building, blithely on my way. Then I hit the end of the ramp which also ends the protection of the building and all heck breaks lose. If I haven't remembered to secure my kite-like cargo, it's off fluttering away and I'm making a mad dash doing a really good scene that would have worked in an "I Love Lucy" show. Papers flying everywhere, bulletin inserts coming apart and sticking to the ground.

Try as I might, I can't possibly keep a hand on the remaining bulletins in the box and catch all the ones in the air or pick up the ones waiting on the ground.

And this has not happened just once to me. Today marked the third time I fell for what looked like calm air. The sun was shining, though the temperature was hovering right at 15 degrees. I only wore my hoodie because I'd been running all over the parish campus all morning and was warm. I escorted my cargo down the ramp and wham, the wind hit it and an instant the air was full of whirling papers.

Only this time it got really bad. Bulletins began flapping through the air across the street, down the next block. I ran inside and screamed for help from my office mates. They came running and it took us quite a few minutes to retrieve bulletins from down the alley and the block.

My fingers were beet red from the wind and my fingernails broken from scratching up paper from concrete. I was exhausted!

All my office companions could do, beside laugh at me was say, "Have you STILL not learned this lesson, Lisa?"

"No," I shake my head, "but I guess I was spreading the Good News! And it was Gone Like the Wind!"

Looking at the Crosses

My newest resolution this year: More chocolate, less angst! Self imposed angst that is, some of it we can't help! "Bear a cross without grumbling" Ack! Why is this so hard sometimes?!!

I'm reminded of Cardinal Dolan who talked about our crosses in his book: "To Whom Shall We Go?

Right now I'm reading the chapter on Embracing the Cross. It couldn't come at a better time. You know how it seems like even though you are trying to do things right in your life, everything is going wrong?

Just yesterday I was musing to God, kind of like Tevye in Fiddler on the Roof does. You know, complaining to God, asking why everything has to keep going wrong all the time, why can't I get a break. Then I sit down to read some of Archbishop Dolan's book and begin the Cross chapter.

That darn golden two-by-four as my hubs calls it, hit me in the head when I read this: "Our Lord could not be more forthright in telling us that the Cross has to be part of discipleship. Why are we so surprised then, when it comes?"

Ouch, he was right. Why am I so surprised when my cross really gets heavy or seems to increase into several crosses. I read further;

Jesus told us it would come. As a matter of fact, when the Cross comes into your life, I propose that it means you're doing something right. You're on the right track. You're actually following our Lord, because He told us the Cross would come."

Now I am picking myself up off the floor because I had just been crabbing at God about how He treats His friends and I thought I was a friend. Here Archbishop is telling me, duh, why do you think you HAVE this cross? Because you ARE friends. " *All of our complaints, our distresses are just different words for the Cross."* Then, lest we think, "Well, it would just be easier if I didn't follow Christ, if I just kind of forgot I knew about the Church and the sacraments, " he goes on to say,

The Cross comes to everybody, whether they are disciples of Christ or not. Everyone experiences the Cross in the simple, ordinary adversities of life.

So, I guess I had better stay friends with Jesus because at least I know he listens and give me comfort through the words of scripture and the sacraments. I always feel better when I've gone to confession and confessed being grumpy with the Lord about my cross!

www.ingramcontent.com/pod-product-compliance
Ingram Content Group UK Ltd.
Pitfield, Milton Keynes, MK11 3LW, UK
UKHW020220250726
13967UKWH00001B/109
9 781304 930644